Growing
Stronger
BASIC

GROWING STRONGER

A handbook for maturing Christians

John C. Souter

Tyndale House
Publishers, Inc.
Wheaton, Illinois

BASIC

OTHER BOOKS BY THE AUTHOR:
Personal Bible Study Notebook Volume 1
Personal Bible Study Notebook Volume 2
Personal Prayer Notebook
Youth Bible Study Notebook
Thessalonians: A Study from The Living Bible
Jesus the Liberator
The Pleasure Seller
Grow! A Handbook for New Christians
How to Grow New Christians
A Family Hour Notebook, Getting to Know God

Unless otherwise noted, all Scripture quotations
are taken from the New American Standard Bible.

Library of Congress Catalog Card Number 79-92172.
ISBN 0-8423-1233-1, paper.
Copyright © 1980 by John C. Souter.
All rights reserved.
First printing, February 1980.
Printed in the United States of America.

CONTENTS

INTRODUCTION

Welcome to <u>Growing Stronger, Basic</u>. It is a tool for you to use as you grow into a true disciple of Jesus Christ. Your discipler will take you through this book one step at a time. Follow his directions carefully and you will build a foundation for becoming an authentic disciple.

This book will be of little value to you unless you have a discipler to lead you through it. (He has a manual too, called <u>How to Grow Strong Christians</u>.) A discipler is a spiritual Christian who has learned to apply the concepts contained in this manual. If you do not have one to work with you, ask your pastor if he can recommend someone who might be willing to help you grow.

There are six sections in this book. Your discipler will take you through this material using projects. Each project will be different. Many involve Bible study, some require memorization of a verse or two, others ask you to learn basic Christian terms. Some projects involve practical activities such as meeting other people and helping them.

You will also read selected chapters from other Christian books and be asked to report on what you learn. Look on these assignments as opportunities to build your personal library with tools that will make you more effective in

God's hands. If money is a problem, try to secure a sponsor to underwrite the cost of buying the books. If it is impossible for you to own them, borrow the books from your church library or from your discipler. The Bible studies in this manual are based on the <u>New American Standard Bible.</u>

Try to meet with your discipler once a week. This may not always be possible, but make it your goal. At each meeting he will go over what you have learned and assign new projects. You will have opportunities to ask questions and share the experience God has brought into your life during the week.

Don't skip ahead in this manual. Do only those tasks that have been assigned. Don't expect to move on to the next section until you have mastered previous material. If there are areas of your life in which you are fighting major sin battles, your discipler will give you additional help. Trust God to use him to bring you to spiritual maturity. Share both your problems and victories with him.

It is not enough to fill out the blanks in this manual. You must develop and practice godlike character to become a true disciple of Jesus Christ. Your goal is to apply the principles from each of the chapters in this book. As you work in this manual, concentrate on coming closer to God

May God richly bless you as you begin this exciting adventure of growing to be like Jesus Christ.

GETTING STARTED

COUNTING THE COST

This manual will cost you. It will cost you hours of hard work, days of spiritual struggle, and months of persistent effort. Before you begin, be like the man who sits down to count the cost. (See Matthew 14:26-35.) Is it worth it? Do you have the time? Are you willing to make the time? Are you willing to sacrifice other things in your schedule so that you will have time? If you love the Lord Jesus and truly want to be his servant, this program is what you need.

Growth takes work, and you may want to give up when the going gets rough. But life's always a struggle. If anything is easy, it is usually not worthwhile. Make up your mind early that you are going to finish this book—that you are going to master its contents.

There will be days when you think that your discipler does not know what he is doing. There will be times when he will ask you to do things you think are a waste of time. But remember, you are asking God to use him to lead you into discipleship, and you can count on the road being rough. Make Ephesians 4:15 your goal: "We are to grow up in all aspects into Him, who is the head, even Christ."

If you are willing to pay the price of true growth, read the following statement in your discipler's presence and make your commitment to God.

COMMITMENT NO. 1
"I have counted the cost of becoming a true disciple of Jesus Christ. I realize that this commitment will cost me time and work. I also realize that there will be times when I will have to sacrifice my own pleasure in order to fulfill this commitment to grow. Before God and my discipler I announce that one of my highest priorities will be time spent in discipleship. I want to grow spiritually and am willing to pay the price for that growth."

_____   _____
(Your Name)   (Discipler)

_____
(Date)

OBEYING SPIRITUAL LEADERS
As you enter into a discipleship relationship with another Christian, you must know that the Bible has much to say about how we are to behave toward those in spiritual authority over us.

"Remember those who led you, who spoke the word of God to you; and considering the outcome of their way of life, imitate their faith. . . . Obey your leaders, and submit to them; for they keep watch over your souls, as those who will give an account. Let them do this with joy and not with grief, for this would be unprofitable for you" (Hebrews 13:7, 17).

Even though your discipler may not be an elder in your church, when you enter into a discipleship arrangement with him he becomes your immediate spiritual authority.

It is God's will that you be submissive to the leadership under which he places you—both secular and spiritual authority. It is not God's will that you allow yourself to be able to complete this manual if you are not subject to his authority. Read and sign Commitment Number 2 in his presence.

COMMITMENT NO. 2
"It is my desire to become a disciple of Jesus Christ. I will submit to the spiritual leadership of the one discipling me and with God's power will do the projects he assigns for my spiritual growth."

_____   _____

(Your Name)   (Discipler)

_____

(Date)

DAILY BIBLE STUDY RECORD
Each day after you study God's Word, list the passage you
studied opposite the correct date below. In this way you
will be able to keep track of your own consistency.

Month _____ Year _____

1 _____	22 _____	11 _____
2 _____	23 _____	12 _____
3 _____	24 _____	13 _____
4 _____	25 _____	14 _____
5 _____	26 _____	15 _____
6 _____	27 _____	16 _____
7 _____	28 _____	17 _____
8 _____	29 _____	18 _____
9 _____	30 _____	19 _____
10 _____	31 _____	20 _____
11 _____	Month _____	21 _____
12 _____	1 _____	22 _____
13 _____	2 _____	23 _____
14 _____	3 _____	24 _____
15 _____	4 _____	25 _____
16 _____	5 _____	26 _____
17 _____	6 _____	27 _____
18 _____	7 _____	28 _____
19 _____	8 _____	29 _____
20 _____	9 _____	30 _____
21 _____	10 _____	31 _____

DAILY BIBLE STUDY RECORD
Each day after you study God's Word, list the passage you
studied opposite the correct date below. In this way you
will be able to keep track of your own consistency.

Month _____ Year _____

1 _____	22 _____	11 _____
2 _____	23 _____	12 _____
3 _____	24 _____	13 _____
4 _____	25 _____	14 _____
5 _____	26 _____	15 _____
6 _____	27 _____	16 _____
7 _____	28 _____	17 _____
8 _____	29 _____	18 _____
9 _____	30 _____	19 _____
10 _____	31 _____	20 _____
11 _____	Month _____	21 _____
12 _____	1 _____	22 _____
13 _____	2 _____	23 _____
14 _____	3 _____	24 _____
15 _____	4 _____	25 _____
16 _____	5 _____	26 _____
17 _____	6 _____	27 _____
18 _____	7 _____	28 _____
19 _____	8 _____	29 _____
20 _____	9 _____	30 _____
21 _____	10 _____	31 _____

DAILY BIBLE STUDY RECORD
Each day after you study God's Word, list the passage you
studied opposite the correct date below. In this way you
will be able to keep track of your own consistency.

Month _____ Year _____

1 _____	22 _____	11 _____
2 _____	23 _____	12 _____
3 _____	24 _____	13 _____
4 _____	25 _____	14 _____
5 _____	26 _____	15 _____
6 _____	27 _____	16 _____
7 _____	28 _____	17 _____
8 _____	29 _____	18 _____
9 _____	30 _____	19 _____
10 _____	31 _____	20 _____
11 _____	Month _____	21 _____
12 _____	1 _____	22 _____
13 _____	2 _____	23 _____
14 _____	3 _____	24 _____
15 _____	4 _____	25 _____
16 _____	5 _____	26 _____
17 _____	6 _____	27 _____
18 _____	7 _____	28 _____
19 _____	8 _____	29 _____
20 _____	9 _____	30 _____
21 _____	10 _____	31 _____

APPOINTMENT SCHEDULE
Use this form to write down each of your appointments with your discipler.

Date	Day	Time	Place

APPOINTMENT SCHEDULE
Use this form to write down each of your appointments
with your discipler.

Date	Day	Time	Place

WEEKLY PROJECTS

Section	Project	Date Given	Date Completed

WEEKLY PROJECTS

Section	Project	Date Given	Date Completed

WEEKLY PROJECTS

Section	Project	Date Given	Date Completed

I

KNOWING CHRIST

INTRODUCTION
Without Christ there is no Christianity. He is at the center
of what we believe because he is God. It is absolutely
essential that you develop a deep personal relationship
with the Lord. It is also extremely important for you to
study God's Word so that you will really know who Jesus
is and what he is like. This section is only a modest
beginning to a lifetime job of knowing Jesus Christ in a
personal way.

Is Jesus Unique to History? "Of the founders of the
world's great religions, one was too lazy to make an honest
living, five had unsuccessful marriages, and at least four
abandoned their wives and children. One was admittedly
disobedient to God while another denied his existence
altogether. Five expressed discouragement at the end of
their lives and considered themselves failures. One
committed murder. Two believed in and practiced violence
to propagate their causes.

"In contrast, Jesus worked with his hands, supporting
his widowed mother until late in his twenty-ninth year. He
never married, and his dealings with women were above
reproach. . . . He stood firmly against violence and stated
that those who live by the sword also die by it. Rather than
defend himself against an accusation which was not true,

he was tortured and executed.

"Jesus claimed to be God. No other great religious liberator in history has made that claim. . . . Every religious founder who is today worshiped as God was considered by his contemporaries to be a normal man. . . . Only the contemporaries of Jesus claimed that he was God. The stories of his deity and resurrection come from those who lived when he was alive. They did not come from followers living centuries after his death. . . .

"There can be no doubt Jesus is on a different level from the rest of mankind. He is unique to history because he alone is God."

John C. Souter
Jesus the Liberator
Tyndale House Publishers

TAKE A LOOK AT YOURSELF
Check every statement that describes your present attitude
toward Christ.   Date_____

☐ 1. I don't really know who Christ is.

☐ 2. I think Jesus is God, but I don't know for sure.

☐ 3. I have a personal relationship with Christ.

☐ 4. I think I have a personal relationship with Christ.

☐ 5. I love the Lord and want to learn more about him.

☐ 6. I have invited Christ into my life.

☐ 7. My consuming desire is to live for the Lord.

☐ 8. I'm just not sure what my relationship with the
        Lord is.

☐ 9. I want to learn exactly what Christianity and Jesus
        are all about.

☐ 10. _____
_____
_____
_____

COMMITMENT NO. 3

"It is my desire _____
_____
_____
_____
_____

_____   _____
(Disciple)   (Discipler)

_____   _____
(Date)   (Date)

BOOK REPORT
Name of Book _____

Author _____ Publisher _____

Chapter(s) read _____

1. Chapter _____ summarized: _____

_____

_____

_____

_____

_____

2. Chapter _____ summarized: _____

_____

_____

_____

_____

_____

3. List important points you should remember: _____

_____

_____

_____

_____

_____

4. What were the most impressive facts you learned? _____

_____

_____

_____

_____

_____

_____

BOOK REPORT
Name of Book _____

Author _____ Publisher _____

Chapter(s) read _____

1. Chapter _____ summarized: _____

_____

_____

_____

_____

_____

2. Chapter _____ summarized: _____

_____

_____

_____

_____

_____

3. List important points you should remember: _____

_____

_____

_____

_____

_____

4. What were the most impressive facts you learned? ____

_____

_____

_____

_____

_____

_____

BIBLE STUDY
Is Jesus God?

Date of Studies_____

1. Look up "deity" in a standard dictionary and write the meaning on the Definition of Terms page in this section.

2. Was it really necessary for Christ to be God? _____

_____

_____

_____

3. List all of the titles for Jesus which call him God in the following references: Isaiah 9:6; Matthew 1:23; 16:16; Luke 1:32; John 1:1; 14:6; Acts 3:14; 10:36; Hebrews 1:10; Revelation 1:8, 17; 19:16.

_____

_____

_____

_____

_____

_____

_____

4. What was Christ claiming in John 8:48-59?_____

_____

_____

_____

5. Why did the Jews try to kill him? _____

_____

_____

6. What divine right did Jesus claim in Matthew 9:2-6?

_____

_____

_____

BIBLE STUDY
Is Jesus God?

Date of Studies_____

7. What divine right did Jesus claim in John 5:22, 27?

_____

_____

_____

8. What divine right did Jesus claim in John 11:25, 26?

_____

_____

_____

9. What is the basic principle taught in Exodus 20:5 and
Matthew 4:10?_____

_____

_____

10. Did Peter follow this principle (Acts 10:25, 26)?_____

_____

_____

_____

11. Why did he and others seem to violate this principle
(Matthew 14:33; 15:25; Luke 5:8; John 20:28)?_____

_____

_____

_____

_____

12. Why didn't Jesus stop these people from breaking a
commandment? _____

_____

_____

_____

BIBLE STUDY
Is Jesus God?

Date of Studies_____

13. If Jesus is God, he must have the same characteristics that God the Father possesses. Listed below are some of the attributes of God. Look up each of the verses describing Christ and place the references opposite the right characteristic. Matthew 9:4; 18:20; 28:18, 20; John 2:24; 3:13; 6:68, 69; 8:58; 13:34; 14:6; 17:5; 18:4; 2 Corinthians 5:21; Hebrews 1:11; 7:26; 13:8; 1 Peter 2:22; 1 John 3:16; Revelation 1:8; 3:7.

Immutability_____

Truth_____

Love_____

Holiness_____

Eternity_____

Omnipresence_____

Omniscience_____

Omnipotence_____
Look up any terms you do not understand.

14. Look up each of the following verses. On the right below, summarize what each says. If you think a verse openly states that Jesus is God, check the box on its left.

☐ Isaiah 9:6_____

☐ John 1:1_____

☐ John 1:18_____

☐ John 20:28_____

☐ Romans 9:5_____

☐ 2 Thessalonians 1:12_____

☐ 1 Timothy 1:17_____

☐ Titus 2:13_____

☐ Hebrews 1:8_____

☐ 2 Peter 1:1_____

☐ 1 John 5:20_____

MEMORY WORK SHEET

Date You Begin Memorizing _____

1. So that you will always know where to locate the verses which specifically state that Jesus is God, write down the references below. (See the last page of your Bible study on "Is Jesus God?")

_____

_____

_____

_____

_____

_____

2. Memorize each reference. (You should also have a good idea what each verse says.)

3. When you're ready, cover the references above and write them in this space:

_____

_____

_____

_____

_____

_____

4. Review the references daily until they are yours. Once you have them memorized, review them every week or two. Record your progress here.

Review date_____Perfect_____Average_____Poor_____

Review date_____Perfect_____Average_____Poor_____

Review date_____Perfect_____Average_____Poor_____

Review date_____Perfect_____Average_____Poor_____

Review date_____Perfect_____Average_____Poor_____

Review date_____Perfect_____Average_____Poor_____

BOOK REPORT
Name of Book _____

Author _____ Publisher _____

Chapter(s) read _____

1. Chapter _____ summarized: _____

_____

_____

_____

_____

_____

2. Chapter _____ summarized: _____

_____

_____

_____

_____

_____

3. List important points you should remember: _____

_____

_____

_____

_____

4. What were the most impressive facts you learned? _____

_____

_____

_____

_____

_____

BOOK REPORT
Name of Book _____

Author _____ Publisher _____

Chapter(s) read _____

1. Chapter _____ summarized: _____

_____

_____

_____

_____

_____

2. Chapter _____ summarized: _____

_____

_____

_____

_____

_____

3. List important points you should remember: _____

_____

_____

_____

_____

_____

4. What were the most impressive facts you learned? _____

_____

_____

_____

_____

_____

BIBLE STUDY
What About the Resurrection?

Date of Studies_____

1. Why is the resurrection important? _____

_____

_____

_____

2. Summarize the teaching in 1 Corinthians 15:12-19._____

_____

_____

_____

_____

There are many references in the Bible which state that
Jesus was raised from the dead. Using cross-references or
a concordance, try to find references to support each of the
following proofs. (Check all four Gospels for each proof.)

3. Christ claimed he would rise from the dead._____

_____

_____

_____

4. Jesus was definitely put to death. _____

_____

_____

_____

5. A heavy stone blocked the entrance to the tomb._____

_____

_____

6. A special seal was attached to the stone. _____

_____

_____

BIBLE STUDY
What About the Resurrection?

Date of Studies_____

7. A guard of soldiers was posted at the tomb. _____

_____

_____

8. The tomb was definitely empty. _____

_____

_____

9. The graveclothes were left behind. _____

_____

_____

10. Jesus made at least twelve appearances to his followers after the resurrection took place. Using the following passages, find as many of those appearances as possible. Summarize the events on the left and place the references to the right of the correct event. (Matthew 28; Mark 16; Luke 24; John 20, 21; Acts 1:1-9; and 1 Corinthians 15:1-8.)

Summary of Event	References
1)	
2)	
3)	
4)	
5)	
6)	
7)	
8)	
9)	
10)	
11)	
12)	

BIBLE STUDY
What About the Resurrection?

Date of Studies_____

Now that you have studied the facts about the resurrection of Christ which are found in the Bible itself, make your own defense to the following four arguments which attempt to disprove the resurrection.

11. "The women merely went to the wrong tomb, and that confused everyone."_____

_____

_____

_____

_____

_____

_____

_____

12. "Jesus was involved in a Passover plot. He plotted his own death and resurrection, but the plot failed and Jesus died. Several impostors faked all of the appearances."

_____

_____

_____

_____

_____

_____

_____

_____

_____

_____

_____

BIBLE STUDY
What About the Resurrection?

Date of Studies_____

13. "There is a completely rational explanation for the empty tomb—somebody stole the body. It was probably the disciples who walked away with the body."

_____

_____

_____

_____

_____

_____

_____

_____

_____

_____

14. "Jesus did not actually die. He swooned, giving the impression that he had died. After meeting with his disciples and convincing them that he had come back to life, he died of his wounds."

_____

_____

_____

_____

_____

_____

_____

_____

_____

MEMORY WORK SHEET

Scripture Reference _____ Date _____

1. Translation to be used: _____

2. Exact passage to be memorized: _____
   _____
   _____
   _____

3. When you're ready, review the passage above and quiz
   yourself by writing it here: _____
   _____
   _____
   _____
   _____
   _____

4. Use this space for a second quiz of the passage:_____
   _____
   _____
   _____
   _____
   _____

5. Each time you review, list the date and check your score:

Review date_____Perfect_____Average_____Poor_____

Review date_____Perfect_____Average_____Poor_____

Review date_____Perfect_____Average_____Poor_____

Review date_____Perfect_____Average_____Poor_____

Review date_____Perfect_____Average_____Poor_____

Review date_____Perfect_____Average_____Poor_____

BIBLE STUDY
Our Relationship with Jesus

Date of Studies_____

1. Paraphrase Philippians 3:8-11.

_____

_____

_____

_____

_____

_____

_____

2. The Amplified Bible translates the first part of verse 10,
"[For my determined purpose is] that I may know Him—
that I may progressively become more deeply and
intimately acquainted with Him, perceiving and
recognizing and understanding [the wonders of His Person]
more strongly and more clearly."

According to this verse, what should your goal be?_____

_____

_____

3. Summarize the content of the following verses:

Galatians 2:20 _____

_____

_____

Colossians 1:27b_____

_____

Romans 8:9, 10 _____

_____

_____

BIBLE STUDY
Our Relationship with Jesus

Date of Studies_____

4. What do the above verses have in common?_____

_____

_____

_____

5. Whom should we live for (2 Corinthians 5:14, 15)? _____

_____

Why? _____

_____

_____

6. What did Christ do for us according to 2 Corinthians
5:19, 21? _____

_____

_____

_____

7. What should begin to happen to us, then, according to
2 Corinthians 5:17? _____

_____

_____

_____

8. What ministry are we given (2 Corinthians 5:18, 20)?

_____

_____

9. How thoroughly is Christ to have control according to
2 Corinthians 10:5? _____

_____

_____

DEFINITION OF TERMS

Jesus of Nazareth—The Jesus of the Bible grew up in the town of Nazareth, in the province of Galilee. The fact that Jesus was from this area convinced many of the religious leaders that he could not be the Messiah (John 7:52). Jesus was, of course, born in Bethlehem of Judea, where the prophets had foretold the Messiah's birth (Micah 5:2).

Christ—The New Testament title meaning, essentially, the "Messiah" or Deliverer of the Jews. "Christ" is not the last name of Jesus.

Messiah—The Old Testament title for the Hebrew Deliverer. He was to come and save Israel from the nations oppressing her. The Jews generally thought of the Messiah as a political deliverer, not a spiritual deliverer.

Deity— _____

_____

_____

Humanity of Jesus—Although Jesus was completely God, he was also completely human. He had a human birth, experienced a human development, and was subject to the sinless problems of man (i.e., he became hungry, thirsty, slept, grew weary, etc.).

Immutability—Unchangeable. The non-moral attribute or characteristic of God which says his essence does not and cannot change. (To change implies improvement or deterioration—neither of which could happen to God because he is already perfect.)

Omnipresence—Everywhere present. The non-moral attribute of God which declares that he can be everywhere at once.

Omnipotence—All-powerful. The non-moral attribute of God which declares he has the power to do anything. This power is subject to his nature, and he therefore cannot contradict himself by sinning or ignoring sin.

Omniscience—All-knowing. The attribute of God which declares that he knows all that can be known—past, present, and future.

Holiness—Absolute purity of being. The chief moral attribute of God which states that he is separate and free from moral evil and sin.

39

PLAN OF ATTACK
Jesus Christ

Date _____

40

PLAN OF ATTACK
Jesus Christ

Date _____

_____

_____

_____

_____

_____

_____

_____

_____

_____

_____

_____

_____

_____

_____

_____

_____

_____

_____

_____

_____

_____

_____

_____

_____

WHAT YOU'VE LEARNED

Date of Quiz_____

What have you learned in this section? This little quiz will give you an opportunity to see how much you've learned while studying the material in this chapter. Don't let this quiz worry you. Its purpose is not to give you a grade, but to show what you've learned. It will let you know in what areas you need work.

1. _____
2. _____
3. _____
4. _____
5. _____
6. _____
7. _____
8. _____
9. _____
10. _____
11. _____
12. _____
13. _____
14. _____
15. _____
16. _____
17. _____
18. _____
   _____
19. _____
   _____
20. _____
   _____

2
YOU AND YOUR BIBLE

INTRODUCTION
The Bible tells us what Christianity is all about. Without it,
we cannot hope to grow into disciples of Christ. This
section introduces you to the character and quality of
God's Word. It is designed to give you a good knowledge
upon which you can build your faith. Your discipler will
also introduce you to books which can build your daily
Bible consistency.

The Importance of the Bible. "Who but God could have
written a book over a period of 2,000 years, in three
different languages, on three continents, by at least 37
individual authors, in 66 parts, and come up with the most
significant Book in history? The Bible is not merely a book,
it is the Book, the Book that from the importance of its
subjects, the wideness of its range, and the majesty of its
Author stands as high above all other books as the heaven
is above the earth.

"Although the Bible is thousands of years old and deals
with many subjects far ahead of the era in which it was
written, it is medically, scientifically, prophetically,
psychologically, and historically accurate. No other book
has inspired so many other books or so much poetry or so
much art. No other book has changed so many lives.

"We are told that the Bible is capable of looking into our

hearts and discerning what is good and what is bad. It is alive. It is constantly active on God's behalf. It is able to teach us what we need to know to live a happy life. It is able to separate us, correct us, feed us, and show us how to develop a God-like personality. In short, the Bible has what we need.

"Have you learned to tap the wisdom in this Book? Has it become the most important Book in your life? You can discover the unbelievable riches in the Bible for yourself. God wrote this Book for you—so that you might live a better life."

John C. Souter
Personal Bible Study Notebook
Tyndale House Publishers

BIBLE STUDY
Authority: Parents and Children

Date of Studies_____

1. Summarize the basic duties of children as you read each of the following Bible passages: Colossians 3:20; Ephesians 6:1-3; Proverbs 6:20-24; 23:22; 28:24; 30:17.

_____

_____

_____

_____

_____

_____

2. Summarize the basic duties of parents as you read each of the following Bible passages: Genesis 18:19; Proverbs 13:24; 19:18; 22:6, 15; 23:13, 14; 29:15, 17; Ephesians 6:4; Colossians 3:21.

_____

_____

_____

_____

_____

_____

3. What does God feel about parents who do not exercise control over their children (1 Samuel 2:12-17, 22-36)?

_____

_____

_____

BIBLE STUDY
Why Study the Bible?

Date of Studies_____

1. The Bible will do many things for you. Look up each of the following references and tell, in your own words, what God's Word can do for you (or what it has already done).

a. James 1:21 (1 Peter 1:23-25)_____

_____

_____

b. 1 John 1:1-4 _____

_____

_____

c. Acts 17:11 _____

_____

d. Hebrews 4:12, 13_____

_____

_____

e. Hebrews 5:13, 14 _____

_____

_____

2. Look up 2 Timothy 3:16, 17. Scripture has four jobs. Define each task.

Teaching:_____

_____

Reproof:_____

_____

Correction:_____

_____

Training:_____

_____

BIBLE STUDY
Bible Study Consistency

Date of Studies_____

1. Read Psalm 119. Note every time David, the psalm writer, refers to God's Word.

2. What was David's attitude toward the Word? _____

_____

_____

3. In Matthew 4:4 Jesus quotes the Old Testament to rebuff Satan. Paraphrase the verse. _____

_____

_____

_____

_____

4. How often do you eat? _____

5. Colossians 3:16 says, "Let the word of Christ richly dwell within you." In practical terms, explain how you can obey this verse.

_____

_____

_____

6. What are you commanded to do in 2 Timothy 2:15? _____

_____

_____

7. Is it possible to obey the passages listed above without some kind of regular intake of God's Word? _____

8. If not, how do you plan to get the Word consistently?

_____

_____

_____

MEMORY WORK SHEET

Scripture Reference _____ Date _____

1. Translation to be used: _____

2. Exact passage to be memorized: _____

_____

_____

_____

3. When you're ready, review the passage above and quiz
yourself by writing it here: _____

_____

_____

_____

_____

4. Use this space for a second quiz of the passage:_____

_____

_____

_____

_____

_____

5. Each time you review, list the date and check your score:

Review date_____Perfect_____Average_____Poor_____

Review date_____Perfect_____Average_____Poor_____

Review date_____Perfect_____Average_____Poor_____

Review date_____Perfect_____Average_____Poor_____

Review date_____Perfect_____Average_____Poor_____

Review date_____Perfect_____Average_____Poor_____

BIBLE STUDY
Inspiration

Date of Studies_____

1. Do you think Peter thought his teachings were inspired?
What about his letters? (See 2 Peter 1:12-15.)_____

_____

_____

_____

2. In verses 16 to 19 of the same chapter Peter describes a
tremendous personal experience: the transfiguration of the
Lord. What was an even stronger evidence for the reality of
this message? (Be certain to look at the note on verse 19 in the
New American Standard Bible.)

_____

_____

_____

_____

3. All Scripture is inspired (2 Timothy 3:16) or "God-
breathed." How did Peter explain the "process" of
inspiration in verses 20 and 21?

_____

_____

_____

4. Did Peter consider Paul's letters to be Scripture
(2 Peter 3:15, 16)? _____

_____

_____

5. What was Christ's attitude toward the Old Testament? See
Matthew 5:17, 18. _____

_____

_____

BIBLE STUDY
Inspiration

Date of Studies_____

6. What three main areas in the Old Testament did Christ teach from in Luke 24:44-47?_____
_____. What do his teachings contain?
_____
_____
_____

7. What did Jesus mean when he made this statement: "The Scripture cannot be broken" (John 10:35)? _____
_____
_____
_____
_____

8. Christ claimed his words could save (Matthew 7:24-29). Why was this so unusual to the crowd? _____
_____
_____
_____

9. What is the Word of God (John 1:1, 14; Revelation 19:13ff.)? _____
_____
_____
_____

10. What is the significance of Christ's taking this title?
_____
_____
_____

BIBLE STUDY
Bible Background

Date of Studies_____

1. How many books are there in the Old Testament?_____
The New Testament? _____ The whole Bible? _____
How many have you read? _____

2. List all of the New Testament authors and write the
number of books each wrote after his name. _____
_____
_____
_____
_____

3. The six types of Bible passages are: Law, History, Poetry,
Prophecy, Gospels, and Epistles. List the type of passage each
of the following books falls into:

John_____   Numbers_____   Joshua_____

Ezekiel_____   Ecclesiastes_____   Hebrews_____

Acts_____   Galatians_____   Proverbs_____

4. What was God's purpose in giving the Law? Check
Galatians 3:15-29. _____
_____
_____
_____

5. How did Christ do away with the Old Testament sacrificial
system? Read Hebrews 10:1-18. _____
_____
_____
_____
_____

PLAN OF ATTACK
Bible Study

Today's Date_____

Your discipler will help you plan your attack.

1. Type of person: _____

2. Best time on weekdays: _____

3. Best time on weekends: _____

4. Possible changes in your routine: _____
_____
_____

5. Alternate Bible study time if change occurs:_____
_____

6. Best place: _____

7. The different types of Bible study.

   a. Devotional books:_____
_____

Advantages:_____
_____

Disadvantages:_____
_____

   b. Directed studies: _____
_____

Advantages:_____
_____

Disadvantages:_____
_____

   c. General questions: _____
_____

Advantages:_____
_____

PLAN OF ATTACK
Bible Study

Disadvantages: _____

_____

   d. Independent Bible study: _____

_____

Advantages: _____

_____

Disadvantages: _____

_____

8. Two basic approaches to Bible study.

   a. Expositional: _____

_____

Advantages: _____

_____

Disadvantages: _____

_____

   b. Topical: _____

_____

Advantages: _____

_____

Disadvantages: _____

_____

9. Basic Bible study guidelines to follow.

   a. Develop consistency: _____

_____

_____

   b. Develop a system: _____

_____

_____

PLAN OF ATTACK
Bible Study

   c. Develop some skills: _____

_____

_____

   d. Develop flexibility: _____

_____

_____

   e. Develop biblical wisdom: _____

_____

_____

   f. Develop depth: _____

_____

_____

   g. Develop a ministry: _____

_____

_____

10. Acquire basic Bible study tools.
   a. Other translations: _____

_____

_____

   b. Concordance: _____

_____

   c. Bible dictionary: _____

_____

_____

   d. Commentary: _____

_____

_____

DEFINITION OF TERMS

Inspiration—The inbreathing of God into men qualifying them to communicate divine truth. The work of God's Spirit in men which enabled them to receive and give divine truth without error.

Verbal Plenary Inspiration—Plenary inspiration teaches that every part of the Bible is equally inspired. Verbal inspiration is the work of God through the Holy Spirit directing Bible writers in their choice of subject matter and words so that they wrote exactly what God desired them to write.

Revelation—The communication of truth that cannot be known apart from a divine source. We believe that this type of revelation has ceased with the closing of the New Testament canon.

Illumination—The light upon the Word of God which every Christian may have from the Holy Spirit. This is not inspiration or revelation. It is only insight into previously revealed truth.

Canon of Scripture—The name given to those geniune, authentic, and inspired books contained in the Bible.

Test of Canonicity—The test by which we have determined which books belong in the Bible:

    a. Divine authorship—Is it inspired?

    b. Human authorship—Was it written by a prophet, or apostle, or spokesman for God?

    c. Genuineness—Can it be traced back to the time and writer from whom it professes to come?

    d. Authenticity—Is it a true record of the facts?

    e. Testimony—Has the book generally been accepted by the Jewish church, the later Christian church, etc.?

WHAT YOU'VE LEARNED

Date of Quiz_____

What have you learned in this section? This little quiz will give you an opportunity to see how much you've learned while studying the material in this chapter. Don't let this quiz worry you. Its purpose is not to give you a grade, but to show what you've learned. It will let you know in what areas you need work.

1. _____

2. _____

3. _____

4. _____

5. _____

6. _____

7. _____

8. _____

9. _____

10. _____

11. _____

12. _____

13. _____

14. _____

15. _____

16. _____

17. _____

18. _____

_____

19. _____

_____

20. _____

_____

3

YOUR PRAYER LIFE-STYLE

INTRODUCTION

I can't think of anything more exciting than to know that the great God of the universe wants to talk to <u>me</u>. But how I have abused this privilege! So often I have been "too busy" to spend time with the most important person in existence.

Because he wants to talk with us, God has created the greatest possible method of communication: prayer. Think for a moment how prayer works. At any moment of the night or day—and you don't even need a transmitter—God is waiting to listen to you. Even when you have to send a "rush message" (like the moment before a car accident), God is always at the other end ready to receive and act upon your prayers.

Some people abuse the privilege of prayer by rudely demanding things of God and considering him to be their personal "answering service." Obviously, the Lord could answer every one of our requests immediately and give us exactly what we want when we want it. But if God were to give you everything you want, how long would you continue to pray? Probably not very long.

God in his wisdom seldom gives us "instant" answers to

our prayers. He encourages us to persevere and labor in conversation with him, because he knows that this relationship is actually more important to our spiritual well-being than the actual answered request will be.

A good prayer life demands time. If you love someone, you want to spend time talking to him. So it is in your relationship with God. If you love him, you will want to make time in your schedule to communicate often with him. This simply cannot be done without a little effort. You must learn to discipline yourself to have a regular time of prayer in which God gets your undivided attention. You must work hard to develop a meaningful prayer life-style that will effectively tap the fantastic resources of spiritual power God wants to release through your requests.

If you are going to have an effective prayer life, you will have to develop a prayer life-style that helps you obey God's Word. This section is designed to guide you into obedience in this very important area of God's Word.

TAKE A LOOK AT YOURSELF

Date_____

Check every statement that describes your present attitude
toward prayer.

☐ 1. I seem never to have any time to pray.

☐ 2. I pray all the time. I don't need one set hour to pray.

☐ 3. I never get any answers when I pray.

☐ 4. I want to pray, but I keep forgetting.

☐ 5. I prayed for something important once and didn't get
it. It's been difficult for me to forgive God for that.

☐ 6. My prayer life is very fruitful.

☐ 7. I am looking forward to learning how to pray better.

☐ 8. _____

_____

_____

_____

COMMITMENT NO. 5

"With the Lord's strength I commit myself to _____

_____

_____

_____

_____

_____   _____
Disciple   Discipler

_____   _____
Date   Date

BIBLE STUDY
When to Pray

Date of Studies_____

1. Jesus gave two parables to communicate an important aspect of prayer. Read both of these stories and summarize the principles they contain.

Luke 11:5-10 _____

_____

_____

Luke 18:1-8 _____

_____

_____

2. At what times and on what occasions did Jesus pray?

a. Matthew 14:23 _____

b. Mark 1:35-38_____

c. Luke 5:15, 16_____

d. Luke 6:12, 13_____

e. Luke 22:39-46 _____

f. John 6:15_____

3. What practical lessons can you draw out of these examples from Jesus' prayer life?_____

_____

_____

_____

4. Paraphrase 1 Thessalonians 5:17 and Ephesians 6:18, 19.

_____

_____

_____

_____

_____

MEMORY WORK SHEET

Scripture Reference_____ Date_____

1. Translation to be used: _____

2. Exact passage to be memorized: _____
_____
_____
_____
_____

3. When you're ready, review the passage above and quiz
yourself by writing it here: _____
_____
_____
_____
_____
_____

4. Use this space for a second quiz of the passage:_____
_____
_____
_____
_____
_____

5. Each time you review, list the date and check your score:

Review date_____Perfect_____Average_____Poor_____
Review date_____Perfect_____Average_____Poor_____
Review date_____Perfect_____Average_____Poor_____
Review date_____Perfect_____Average_____Poor_____
Review date_____Perfect_____Average_____Poor_____
Review date_____Perfect_____Average_____Poor_____

BIBLE STUDY
Balanced Praying

Date of Studies_____

1. The five elements of prayer are worship, thanksgiving, confession, intercession, and petition. What are your

weakest areas? _____

_____

Why?_____

_____

2. Read John 4:23, 24. What does worshiping in spirit and

truth mean?_____

_____

_____

_____

3. Why can't you worship God when you're not in fellowship —when you're carnal (Psalm 66:18)? _____

_____

_____

_____

4. How are we able to understand the things of the Spirit, according to 1 Corinthians 2:9-16? _____

_____

_____

_____

5. What do you feel is involved in the process of worship? What must take place in your heart? _____

_____

_____

_____

Have your own meaningful time of worship right now.

BIBLE STUDY
Praise-Thanksgiving

Date of Studies_____)_____

6. Look up and summarize the teachings on thanksgiving found in 1 Thessalonians 5:17, 18 and Philippians 4:6. _____

_____

_____

_____

_____

7. Why is it a sacrifice to praise God (Hebrews 13:15)? _____

_____

_____

8. What are some of the things you can thank God for?_____

_____

_____

_____

9. Read Psalm 150. Spend a few minutes meditating on verse 6. Write out all the types of life that you can think of that this passage is talking about.

_____

_____

_____

_____

_____

10. Like the psalmist, write your own song to God. Praise him for who he is: _____

_____

_____

_____

_____

63

BIBLE STUDY
Confession

Date of Studies_____

11. Read Isaiah 1:11-16. These people were doing what God told them to. Why was he displeased? _____

_____

_____

12. How did God want them to change? _____

_____

_____

13. Read Psalm 51 and break it down into a rough outline. Summarize the basic things David is asking God:_____

_____

_____

_____

_____

_____

_____

_____

_____

14. What are the teachings on confession revealed in Isaiah 59:1, 2 and 1 John 1:7, 0? _____

_____

_____

_____

_____

15. On a separate piece of paper, write every unconfessed sin or bad attitude that you have not already confessed. After you have admitted each problem area to God, write 1 John 1:9 over these sins. Destroy the paper when you are done.

BIBLE STUDY
Intercession-Petition

Date of Studies_____

16. Summarize the teachings on intercession found in the following verses:

a. Ephesians 6:18, 19 _____

_____

b. 1 Timothy 2:1-4_____

_____

c. James 5:16_____

_____

17. Summarize the teachings on petition found in the following verses:

a. Romans 8:26, 27 _____

_____

b. Philippians 4:6_____

_____

c. James 4:2, 3 _____

_____

18. What is the difference between intercession and petition? _____

_____

_____

19. List some non-Christians you want to pray for: _____

_____

20. List some Christians you want to pray for: _____

_____

_____

21. List your own prayer needs: _____

_____

_____

65

BIBLE STUDY
Getting Answers

Date of Studies_____

1. What are the conditions for answered prayer, according to these verses?

a. Psalm 37:4, 5_____

_____

b. John 15:16_____

_____

c. John 16:23, 24 _____

_____

d. James 1:5-8 _____

_____

e. 1 John 3:22_____

_____

f. 1 John 5:14, 15 _____

_____

2. How can you know if something is God's will? _____

_____

_____

3. How can you determine if your prayer request is selfish or not (James 4:3; Hebrews 4:12, 13)?_____

_____

_____

_____

4. How can you "let the peace of Christ rule in your hearts" (Colossians 3:15a)?_____

_____

_____

_____

66

PLAN OF ATTACK
Prayer Life-Style

Your discipler will help you plan your attack. Date_____

1. Established time on weekdays: _____

2. Established time on weekends: _____

3. Basic prayer guidelines to follow.

  a. Developing consistency:_____

_____

_____

  b. Developing a system: _____

_____

_____

  c. Developing some skills: _____

_____

_____

  d. Developing flexibility:_____

_____

  e. Developing depth:_____

_____

_____

  f. Developing a ministry:_____

_____

_____

4. Acquiring basic prayer tools.

  a. An organized list:_____

_____

  b. A prayer diary:_____

_____

  c. A place to record answered prayer:_____

_____

WHAT YOU'VE LEARNED

Date of Quiz_____

What have you learned in this section? This little quiz will
give you an opportunity to see how much you've learned
while studying the material in this chapter. Don't let this
quiz worry you. Its purpose is not to give you a grade, but
to show what you've learned. It will let you know in what
areas you need work.

1. _____
2. _____
3. _____
4. _____
5. _____
6. _____
7. _____
8. _____
9. _____
10. _____
11. _____
12. _____
13. _____
14. _____
15. _____
16. _____
17. _____
18. _____
_____
19. _____
_____
20. _____
_____

YOU BELONG IN THE BODY

INTRODUCTION
The Bible establishes the Church as the official
organization of God on earth. The Church is the center of
God's will for the growth and development of his Body. The
Church is the Body of Christ on earth. It is through
fellowshipping with other believers that you will be
challenged to grow spiritually. All Christians need a
church-home. This section will help you grow in this
important area.

Love and Affection in the Body. "Bob Wheeler, a carpenter
by trade, was the person who led me to Christ many years
ago. One of the most significant things he did was to
involve me in his family life. His home was my home. I
always felt welcome. I cannot recall how many times I ate
at his table, but I know I virtually ate him out of house
and home!

"There is a certain chemistry that takes place in the
fellowship of believers which produces an environment
that is conducive for growth and stability. I can remember
when Bob took me to church for the first time. His friends
became my friends. The fellowship and encouragement

they showed me was a major factor in my development as a Christian.

"Church was where I had an opportunity to observe other believers and adopt their life-style as mine. There was a great deal in my old life that had to be discarded, and a great deal of my new life that had to be incorporated. That small church played a major role in my making that transition."

Walter A. Henrichsen
Disciples Are Made—Not Born
Victor Books

TAKE A LOOK AT YOURSELF

Date _____

Check every statement that describes your present attitude toward the Body of believers.

☐ 1. I don't really enjoy going to church.

☐ 2. You can be a Christian without going to church.

☐ 3. I don't get enough fellowship at church.

☐ 4. I don't know the people at church.

☐ 5. I don't get anything out of church.

☐ 6. I really enjoy meeting with other Christians.

☐ 7. I can't get enough of the teaching of the Word.

☐ 8. I love the teaching at my church.

☐ 9. I don't have a church home.

☐ 10. I have a good church home.

☐ 11. _____

_____

COMMITMENT NO. 6

"With the Lord's strength I commit myself to _____

_____

_____

_____

_____

_____   _____
Disciple   Discipler

_____   _____
Date   Date

BIBLE STUDY
Life in the Body

Date of Studies_____

1. What activities did the first band of believers engage in according to Acts 2:42-47? _____

_____

_____

_____

_____

_____

2. How important is regular fellowship together according to Hebrews 10:24, 25? _____

_____

_____

3. What other activities go along with the fellowship? _____

_____

_____

4. How important is the Word to the Body (Acts 17:11)?

_____

_____

_____

5. What principles of fellowship are contained in Romans 15:5-7? _____

_____

_____

_____

6. What principle is contained in 1 Corinthians 10:24, 33?

_____

_____

_____

BIBLE STUDY
Composition of the Body

Date of Studies_____

Look up 1 Corinthians 12:12-31 and summarize all the
principles this passage contains about the Body, the Church.

Summary	**Verse**

BIBLE STUDY
Building the Body

Date of Studies_____

1. What is the chief characteristic that should describe Christian fellowship to the world (John 13:34, 35)?_____

_____

_____

2. What do you think is the difference between Christian fellowship and simple Christian friendship?_____

_____

_____

_____

3. In the first column below, list the principles of fellowship found in Philippians 2:1-5. In the second column, list how they can be applied to daily life.

Principles   **Application**

_____

_____

_____

_____

_____

_____

_____

_____

_____

_____

_____

_____

_____

_____

MEMORY WORK SHEET

Scripture Reference _____ Date _____

1. Translation to be used: _____

2. Exact passage to be memorized: _____
_____
_____
_____
_____

3. When you're ready, review the passage above and quiz
yourself by writing it here: _____
_____
_____
_____
_____
_____

4. Use this space for a second quiz of the passage:_____
_____
_____
_____
_____
_____

5. Each time you review, list the date and check your score:

Review date_____Perfect_____Average_____Poor_____
Review date_____Perfect_____Average_____Poor_____
Review date_____Perfect_____Average_____Poor_____
Review date_____Perfect_____Average_____Poor_____
Review date_____Perfect_____Average_____Poor_____
Review date_____Perfect_____Average_____Poor_____

BIBLE STUDY
Growing in the Body

Date of Studies_____

1. We are told to bear one another's burdens in Galatians 6:2 and Romans 15:1, 2. What do you think this means?

_____

_____

_____

2. Can you think of tangible ways in which people in your church have supported other believers through their problems?

_____

_____

_____

3. We are instructed to confess our faults to one another in James 5:16. Why do you think we are to reveal our problems so openly to other Christians?

_____

_____

_____

4. Is it difficult for you to open up and admit your faults to other believers? _____

_____

_____

5. If you were in a growth group of believers who practiced the principles of love contained in 1 Corinthians 13:4-7, do you think it would be easier to open up?

_____

_____

6. Do you practice those principles of love? _____

_____

_____

BOOK REPORT
Name of Book _____

Author _____ Publisher _____

Chapter(s) read _____

1. Chapter_____summarized:_____
_____
_____
_____
_____
_____

2. Chapter _____ summarized:_____
_____
_____
_____
_____
_____

3. List important points you should remember: _____
_____
_____
_____
_____
_____

4. What were the most impressive facts you learned?_____
_____
_____
_____
_____
_____
_____

PLAN OF ATTACK
In the Body

Date _____

Your discipler will help you plan your attack.

1. What Body of believers do you (or will you) fellowship with: _____

_____

2. Membership:_____

_____

3. Baptism: _____

_____

4. List all of the meetings (excluding socials) which you could attend on a regular basis: _____

_____

_____

_____

_____

_____

5. Your commitment to the Body:_____

_____

_____

_____

_____

6. Your commitment to certain members in the Body:

Person   **Ministry**

_____

_____

_____

_____

WHAT YOU'VE LEARNED

Date of Quiz_____

What have you learned in this section? This little quiz will give you an opportunity to see how much you've learned while studying the material in this chapter. Don't let this quiz worry you. Its purpose is not to give you a grade, but to show what you've learned. It will let you know in what areas you need work.

1. _____

2. _____

3. _____

4. _____

5. _____

6. _____

7. _____

8. _____

9. _____

10. _____

11. _____

12. _____

13. _____

14. _____

15. _____

16. _____

17. _____

18. _____

_____

19. _____

_____

20. _____

_____

5

GET UNDER
THE SPIRIT'S POWER

INTRODUCTION

Nineteen and a half centuries ago a handful of men and women—followers of an obscure Galilean prophet—shook the very foundation of world paganism. Thousands upon thousands were won to faith in Jesus Christ. When the Apostle Paul wrote his letter to the church at Rome, Christianity had already penetrated into the imperial household.

What was the secret of such results? Where did these early Christians get their power? Why were they so successful? The Book of Acts and ancient history both agree that these early disciples had a fearless spiritual power like nothing the world had ever seen before. They were filled with the very fullness of God (Ephesians 3:19).

When reading the Book of Acts you can't help but feel the exhilaration of the spiritual power these men and women experienced. It is a power which is foreign to many modern-day Christians. But, praise God, his power is for the Christian in our generation too—and he wants us to experience that power now.

We must always be careful that we don't force the Word of God to fit our experience—or lack of experience. Our goal should always be to let the New Testament establish our spiritual experience. We must always let God be God. He wants to bless each of us with the power to do his will here on earth. This chapter will help you explore what the Bible teaches on the filling of the Holy Spirit.

Being Filled with the Holy Spirit. "The most important thing in the life of any Christian is to be filled with the Holy Spirit! The Lord Jesus said, 'Without Me ye can do nothing.' Christ is in believers in the person of His Holy Spirit. Therefore, if we are filled with His Spirit, He works fruitfully through us. If we are not filled with the Holy Spirit, we are unproductive.

"It is almost impossible to exaggerate how dependent we are on the Holy Spirit. We are dependent on Him for convicting us of sin before and after our salvation, for giving us understanding of the Gospel, causing us to be born again, empowering us to witness, guiding us in our prayer life—in fact, for everything."

Tim LaHaye
Spirit-Controlled Temperament
Tyndale House Publishers

TAKE A LOOK AT YOURSELF

Date _____

Check every statement that describes your present attitude toward God's Spirit.

☐ 1. I'm not really sure when I'm filled by the Spirit.

☐ 2. I'm filled with the Spirit often.

☐ 3. I'd like to live a more consistent Spirit-filled life.

☐ 4. I don't really know what it means to be filled.

☐ 5. I want to develop the fruit of the Spirit.

☐ 6. My spiritual life has been like a roller coaster ride.

☐ 7. I'm still struggling with major sin problems.

☐ 8. I'm anxious to get everything God wants to give me.

☐ 9. _____

☐10. _____

_____

_____

COMMITMENT NO. 7

"It is my desire to: _____

_____

_____

_____

_____   _____
(Disciple)   (Discipler)

_____   _____
(Date)   (Date)

BIBLE STUDY
Who Is the Holy Spirit?

Date of Studies_____

1. What works does the Holy Spirit perform which only God can perform? _____

   a. Genesis 1:2, 26; Psalm 104:30 _____

_____

_____

   b. 2 Peter 1:20, 21_____

_____

_____

   c. Luke 1:35 _____

_____

   d. Acts 2:2-4 _____

_____

_____

2. In what way do the following verses indicate that the Holy Spirit is God?

   a. Jeremiah 31:31-34; Hebrews 10:15-17 _____

_____

_____

   b. Matthew 28:19 _____

_____

_____

   c. Mark 3:28, 29_____

_____

_____

   d. 1 Corinthians 6:19 _____

_____

_____

BIBLE STUDY
Ministry of the Holy Spirit

Date of Studies_____

1. What are some of the ministries of the Holy Spirit?
   a. John 16:13-15 _____

   _____

   _____

   b. Romans 8:12, 13 _____

   _____

   _____

   c. Romans 8:26, 27 _____

   _____

   _____

   d. 1 Corinthians 12:3 _____

   _____

   _____

   e. 1 Peter 1:2 _____

   _____

   _____

2. In John 16:8-11, how and why will the Spirit convict?
   a. Conviction of sin (v. 9)_____

   _____

   _____

   b. Conviction of righteousness (v. 10)_____

   _____

   _____

   c. Conviction of judgment (v. 11) _____

   _____

   _____

BIBLE STUDY
Ministry of the Holy Spirit

Date of Studies_____

3. How is the presence of the Holy Spirit a proof that someone has become a Christian?

 a. Romans 8:9_____

_____

 b. Romans 8:14-16 _____

_____

_____

 c. 1 John 3:24; 4:13 _____

_____

_____

4. Summarize the regenerating ministry of the Spirit in the following verses:

 a. Ephesians 1:13, 14 _____

_____

_____

 b. 1 Thessalonians 4:7, 8_____

_____

_____

 c. 2 Thessalonians 2:13 _____

_____

_____

 d. Titus 3:5 _____

_____

5. In the context of Ephesians 4:25-32 how would you say the Holy Spirit is grieved? _____

_____

_____

MEMORY WORK SHEET

Scripture Reference _____ Date _____

1. Translation to be used: _____

2. Exact passage to be memorized: _____
_____
_____
_____
_____

3. When you're ready, review the passage above and quiz yourself by writing it here: _____
_____
_____
_____
_____
_____

4. Use this space for a second quiz of the passage:_____
_____
_____
_____
_____
_____

5. Each time you review, list the date and check your score:

Review date_____Perfect_____Average_____Poor_____
Review date_____Perfect_____Average_____Poor_____
Review date_____Perfect_____Average_____Poor_____
Review date_____Perfect_____Average_____Poor_____
Review date_____Perfect_____Average_____Poor_____
Review date_____Perfect_____Average_____Poor_____

BIBLE STUDY
Filling of the Spirit

Date of Studies_____

1. What does it mean to be filled with the Spirit, according to
Ephesians 5:18-21? Analyze each phrase. _____

_____

_____

_____

_____

2. What is the purpose of being filled with the Holy Spirit in
the following verses?

   a. Acts 4:8-12_____

_____

_____

   b. Acts 4:31_____

_____

_____

   c. Acts 9:17-22 _____

_____

_____

   d. Acts 13:9-12 _____

_____

_____

   e. Acts 13:48-52_____

_____

_____

3. What do the "rivers of living water" mean in
John 7:37-39?_____

_____

_____

PLAN OF ATTACK
Filling of the Spirit

Date _____

_____

_____

_____

_____

_____

_____

_____

_____

_____

_____

_____

_____

_____

_____

_____

_____

_____

_____

_____

_____

_____

_____

_____

_____

BOOK REPORT
Name of Book _____

Author _____ Publisher _____

Chapter(s) read _____

1. Chapter _____ summarized: _____
_____
_____
_____
_____
_____

2. Chapter _____ summarized: _____
_____
_____
_____
_____
_____

3. List important points you should remember: _____
_____
_____
_____
_____
_____

4. What were the most impressive facts you learned? _____
_____
_____
_____
_____
_____

BOOK REPORT
Name of Book _____

Author _____ Publisher _____

Chapter(s) read _____

1. Chapter_____summarized:_____

_____

_____

_____

_____

_____

2. Chapter _____ summarized:_____

_____

_____

_____

_____

_____

3. List important points you should remember: _____

_____

_____

_____

_____

_____

4. What were the most impressive facts you learned?_____

_____

_____

_____

_____

_____

_____

BIBLE STUDY
Walking in the Spirit

Date of Studies_____

1. What is the result of walking in the Spirit, according to Galatians 5:16? _____

_____

_____

_____

2. What must you do to walk in the Spirit, according to Galatians 5:17? _____

_____

_____

_____

3. What is the difference between living by the Spirit and walking by the Spirit (Galatians 5:25)?_____

_____

_____

_____

_____

4. If you belong to Jesus, exactly what should you do, according to Galatians 5:24? _____

_____

_____

_____

5. How do you get the fruit of the Spirit (Galatians 5:22, 23)?

_____

_____

_____

_____

BIBLE STUDY
Spirit-Controlled Living

Date of Studies_____

Examine Romans 8:1-13 and list every principle of Spirit-controlled living found in the passage. Place the principle on the left and the references on the right.

Principle	Verse

92

PLAN OF ATTACK
Walking in the Spirit

Date _____

_____

_____

_____

_____

_____

_____

_____

_____

_____

_____

_____

_____

_____

_____

_____

_____

_____

_____

_____

_____

_____

_____

_____

_____

WHAT YOU'VE LEARNED

Date of Quiz_____

What have you learned in this section? This little quiz will give you an opportunity to see how much you've learned while studying the material in this chapter. Don't let this quiz worry you. Its purpose is not to give you a grade, but to show what you've learned. It will let you know in what areas you need work.

1. _____
2. _____
3. _____
4. _____
5. _____
6. _____
7. _____
8. _____
9. _____
10. _____
11. _____
12. _____
13. _____
14. _____
15. _____
16. _____
17. _____
18. _____
_____
19. _____
_____
20. _____
_____

6

OVERCOMING TEMPTATION

INTRODUCTION

Every Christian is faced with temptation. Many would-be disciples are sidelined every day because they fall into one or two areas of major sin. If you want to grow into a true disciple, you must know what temptation is and how to handle it. This chapter will give you practical help at becoming an "overcomer."

Temptation. "Temptation is common to man. Or as <u>The Living New Testament</u> expresses it: 'But remember this—the wrong desires that come into your life aren't anything new and different. Many others have faced exactly the same problems before you' (1 Cor. 10:13). . . .

"But to read or hear some on the spiritual life, one would think that the so-called victorious Christian never experiences temptation; or if he does, it is a slight and fleeting experience which really causes him no problem. I have just made a perusal of a half dozen books on the spiritual life. Only one of them mentioned temptation and then in only two paragraphs. Perhaps this unrealistic attitude toward the reality of temptation is the cause of discouragement among some believers who, thinking they have the 'secret' of victory, suddenly find themselves not only confronted with temptation but actually overcome by it.

"But, while temptation is common to man, the believer does not have to yield to it, for God in His mercy makes ways to escape so that we can bear it. Thus the believer, though never free from exposure to temptation, need not succumb to it. Indeed, spiritual believers are the more confronted with temptation."

Charles Caldwell Ryrie
Balancing the Christian Life
Moody Press

RESOURCE SHEET

There is within each of us a natural curiosity to know about evil. Look at the most popular newspaper stories; murder, bizarre acts of violence, and sex crimes hold a strange fascination for most of us. Of course we're disgusted by such corruption—but why do we still have such strong desires to know about its existence?

We often read about the sins and excesses of others, telling ourselves that the knowledge will make us "better able to help them." We rationalize that the exaggerated acts of sex and violence on our TV and movie screens don't affect us—when in reality we are becoming increasingly hardened to these realistic simulations of evil.

King David was honest enough to admit that he had secretly envied corrupt men. Who can say that deep down within his heart there is not a tremendous possibility and desire for sin? But as long as we toy with sin, it will be increasingly easy for us to fall prey to temptation.

The Bible makes it extremely clear that we are to stay as far away from evil as possible. "I want you to be wise in what is good, and innocent in what is evil" (Romans 16:19b). ". . . in evil be babes, but in your thinking be mature" (1 Corinthians 14:20b).

We must learn to shelter our minds from moral garbage and build in them spiritual purity. "We are destroying speculations and every lofty thing raised up against the knowledge of God, and we are taking every thought captive to the obedience of Christ" (2 Corinthians 10:5).

COMMITMENT NO. 8

"With the Lord's strength I commit myself to: _____

_____

_____

_____   _____
Disciple   Discipler

_____   _____
Date   Date

BIBLE STUDY
Purpose of Temptation

Date of Studies_____

Every trial comes for one of two reasons: either it is a testing from God for your good, or it is designed by Satan to corrupt you. Summarize the content in each of the following verses.

1. Examples of beneficial testing:

Hebrews 12:1-13_____

_____

_____

James 1:2-4_____

_____

_____

1 Peter 1:6, 7_____

_____

_____

1 Peter 4:12, 13_____

_____

_____

2. Examples of temptation designed to corrupt:

Luke 8:13_____

_____

1 Timothy 6:9_____

_____

_____

3. We are also commanded to pray and take careful watch to avoid falling into temptation by our own carelessness. Examine Matthew 6:13 and 26:41. What do they say?

_____

_____

98

BIBLE STUDY
Promises about Temptation

Date of Studies_____

"No temptation has overtaken you but such as is common
to man; and God is faithful, who will not allow you to be
tempted beyond what you are able; but with the temptation
will provide the way of escape also, that you may be able to
endure it" (1 Corinthians 10:13).

Summarize the content in each of the following passages:

1. No unusual temptations—they are common to other
Christians.

1 John 1:8, 10 _____

_____

_____

James 3:2 _____

_____

_____

Hebrews 4:15 _____

_____

_____

2. God is faithful.

Malachi 3:6 _____

_____

_____

Romans 3:3, 4 _____

_____

_____

1 Corinthians 1:9_____

_____

_____

1 John 1:9_____

_____

BIBLE STUDY
Promises about Temptation

Date of Studies_____

3. You won't be tempted beyond what you can handle.

James 1:13 _____

_____

_____

Hebrews 4:15a, 16_____

_____

_____

4. God will always provide an escape.

Hebrews 2:18 _____

_____

_____

2 Peter 2:9_____

_____

_____

5. You will be able to endure (with his help).

1 Thessalonians 5:23_____

_____

_____

2 Thessalonians 3:3 _____

_____

_____

1 Peter 1:5_____

_____

_____

1 John 5:18 (Amplified) _____

_____

_____

MEMORY WORK SHEET

Scripture Reference _____ Date _____

1. Translation to be used: _____

2. Exact passage to be memorized: _____

_____

_____

_____

_____

3. When you're ready, review the passage above and quiz yourself by writing it here: _____

_____

_____

_____

_____

_____

4. Use this space for a second quiz of the passage:_____

_____

_____

_____

_____

_____

5. Each time you review, list the date and check your score:

Review date_____Perfect_____Average_____Poor_____

Review date_____Perfect_____Average_____Poor_____

Review date_____Perfect_____Average_____Poor_____

Review date_____Perfect_____Average_____Poor_____

Review date_____Perfect_____Average_____Poor_____

Review date_____Perfect_____Average_____Poor_____

BIBLE STUDY
Levels of Temptation

Date of Studies_____

Listed below are the four stages of temptation.

1. Stage 1—<u>The Evil Heart</u>. Paraphrase the two passages below.

Mark 7:20-23 _____

_____

_____

_____

Matthew 12:34, 35_____

_____

_____

_____

2. Stage 2—<u>Lust</u>. Summarize the verses below:

James 1:14 _____

_____

_____

Romans 8:7, 8 _____

_____

_____

Ephesians 2:3 _____

_____

_____

3. Stage 3—<u>Sin</u>. Summarize the verses below.

James 1:15a_____

_____

Romans 3:23 _____

_____

BIBLE STUDY
Levels of Temptation

Date of Studies_____

4. Stage 4—<u>Death</u>. Paraphrase each reference below.

Romans 6:23 _____

_____

Romans 8:6-8 _____

_____

_____

Romans 7:5 _____

_____

James 1:15b_____

_____

5. In Matthew 5:29, 30 Jesus indicated that if one of your eyes caused you to sin you should pluck it out. Is it your eye that causes the sin?

_____

_____

_____

6. In Matthew 6:22, 23 Jesus reveals the fact that the eye-gate is very important. What do you feel he is saying?

_____

_____

7. Are the eyes ever satisfied (Proverbs 27:20)? _____

_____

_____

8. What did Job do to overcome the possible problems that could be stimulated through the eyes (Job 31:1)?_____

_____

_____

BIBLE STUDY
Sin Areas

Date of Studies_____

1. Carefully read 1 John 2:15-17.

   a. What are we not to do?_____

_____

   b. What is happening to the evil world? _____

_____

_____

   c. List each of the three sin areas described in verse 16, then define the meaning of each.

   1)_____

_____

_____

   2)_____

_____

_____

   3)_____

_____

_____

2. Look up the deeds of the flesh listed in Galatians 5:19-21. Put each sin under the proper sin area below (taken from above).

   a._____

_____

   b._____

_____

   c._____

_____

TAKE A LOOK AT YOURSELF

Date_____

Take a close look at each of the major sin areas below and check off areas in which you receive heavy temptation.

1. <u>Moral Impurity</u>

☐ Lustful thoughts   ☐ An alcohol problem

☐ Lustful actions   ☐ Major immorality

☐ Overeating   ☐ A drug problem

☐ Bad habits   ☐ _____

☐ Pride because of appearance

2. <u>Wrong Values</u> (Materialism)

☐ Desiring to be rich   ☐ Laziness

☐ Desiring to possess things   ☐ Pride because of looks

☐ Desiring to possess people   ☐ Jealousy

☐ Overspending   ☐ Miserly attitudes

☐ Being selfish   ☐ _____

☐ Pride because of possessions

3. <u>The Pride of Life</u> (Bitterness)

☐ Sarcasm   ☐ Unloving spirit

☐ Slander   ☐ Untruthfulness

☐ Gossip   ☐ Lack of love

☐ Cutting remarks   ☐ _____

☐ Unforgiving spirit   ☐ _____

4. In which areas do you find yourself under greatest attack? _____

_____

_____

_____

_____

BOOK REPORT
Name of Book _____

Author _____ Publisher _____

Chapter(s) read _____

1. Chapter _____ summarized: _____
_____
_____
_____
_____
_____

2. Chapter _____ summarized: _____
_____
_____
_____
_____
_____

3. List important points you should remember: _____
_____
_____
_____
_____
_____

4. What were the most impressive facts you learned? _____
_____
_____
_____
_____
_____
_____

PLAN OF ATTACK
Temptation

Date_____

<u>First Line of Defense</u> (Before You Are Exposed to the Temptation)

1._____
_____
_____
_____
_____
_____

2._____
_____
_____
_____
_____
_____

3._____
_____
_____
_____
_____
_____

4._____
_____
_____
_____
_____
_____

PLAN OF ATTACK
Temptation

Date_____

<u>Second Line of Defense</u> (Once You Are Faced with the Actual Temptation)

1. Incorrect Responses: _____

_____

_____

_____

_____

_____

_____

_____

_____

_____

_____

2. Correct Responses: _____

_____

_____

_____

_____

_____

_____

_____

_____

_____

_____

PLAN OF ATTACK
Temptation

Date_____

<u>Third Line of Defense</u> (After You Have Fallen to the
Temptation)

1. Incorrect Responses: _____

_____

_____

_____

_____

2. Correct Responses: _____

   a._____

_____

_____

   b._____

_____

_____

   c._____

_____

_____

   d._____

_____

_____

3. Using Your Sin:_____

_____

_____

_____

_____

WHAT YOU'VE LEARNED

Date of Quiz_____

What have you learned in this section? This little quiz will
give you an opportunity to see how much you've learned
while studying the material in this chapter. Don't let this
quiz worry you. Its purpose is not to give you a grade, but
to show what you've learned. It will let you know in what
areas you need work.

1. _____
2. _____
3. _____
4. _____
5. _____
6. _____
7. _____
8. _____
9. _____
10. _____
11. _____
12. _____
13. _____
14. _____
15. _____
16. _____
17. _____
18. _____

19. _____

20. _____

WHAT YOU'VE LEARNED
Final

Date of Final_____

What have you learned through taking this course? This
final will give you an opportunity to see how much you've
learned while studying the material in this book. The
purpose of this final is not to grade you, but to give you an
opportunity to see what you need to work on.

1. _____	26. _____
2. _____	27. _____
3. _____	28. _____
4. _____	29. _____
5. _____	30. _____
6. _____	31. _____
7. _____	32. _____
8. _____	33. _____
9. _____	34. _____
10. _____	35. _____
11. _____	36. _____
12. _____	37. _____
13. _____	38. _____
14. _____	39. _____
15. _____	40. _____
16. _____	41. _____
17. _____	42. _____
18. _____	43. _____
19. _____	44. _____
20. _____	45. _____
21. _____	46. _____
22. _____	47. _____
23. _____	48. _____
24. _____	49. _____
25. _____	50. _____

MEMORY WORK SHEET

Scripture Reference _____ Date _____

1. Translation to be used: _____

2. Exact passage to be memorized: _____

_____

_____

_____

_____

3. When you're ready, review the passage above and quiz yourself by writing it here: _____

_____

_____

_____

_____

_____

4. Use this space for a second quiz of the passage:_____

_____

_____

_____

_____

_____

5. Each time you review, list the date and check your score:

Review date_____Perfect_____Average_____Poor_____

Review date_____Perfect_____Average_____Poor_____

Review date_____Perfect_____Average_____Poor_____

Review date_____Perfect_____Average_____Poor_____

Review date_____Perfect_____Average_____Poor_____

Review date_____Perfect_____Average_____Poor_____

MEMORY WORK SHEET

Scripture Reference _____ Date _____

1. Translation to be used: _____

2. Exact passage to be memorized: _____

_____

_____

_____

_____

3. When you're ready, review the passage above and quiz
yourself by writing it here: _____

_____

_____

_____

_____

_____

4. Use this space for a second quiz of the passage:_____

_____

_____

_____

_____

_____

5. Each time you review, list the date and check your score:

Review date_____Perfect_____Average_____Poor_____

Review date_____Perfect_____Average_____Poor_____

Review date_____Perfect_____Average_____Poor_____

Review date_____Perfect_____Average_____Poor_____

Review date_____Perfect_____Average_____Poor_____

Review date_____Perfect_____Average_____Poor_____